I0447024

*Congressional
Research
Service*

The American Opportunity Tax Credit: Overview, Analysis, and Policy Options

Margot L. Crandall-Hollick
Analyst in Public Finance

June 11, 2012

Congressional Research Service
7-5700
www.crs.gov
R42561

CRS Report for Congress
Prepared for Members and Committees of Congress

Summary

The American Opportunity Tax Credit (AOTC)—enacted on a temporary basis by the American Recovery and Reinvestment Act (ARRA; P.L. 111-5) and extended through the end of 2012 by the Tax Relief, Unemployment Insurance Reauthorization, and Job Creation Act of 2010 (P.L. 111-312)—is a partially refundable tax credit that provides financial assistance to taxpayers who are attending college, or whose children are attending college. The credit, worth up to $2,500 per student, can be claimed for a student's first four years of post-secondary education. In addition, 40% of the credit (up to $1,000) can be received as a refund by taxpayers with little or no tax liability. The credit phases out for taxpayers with income between $80,000 and $90,000 ($160,000 and $180,000 for married couples filing jointly) and is hence unavailable to taxpayers with income above $90,000 ($180,000 for married couples filing jointly). There are a variety of other eligibility requirements associated with the AOTC, including the type of degree the student is pursuing, the number of courses the student is taking, and the type of expenses which qualify.

Prior to the enactment of the AOTC, there were two permanent education tax credits, the Hope Credit and the Lifetime Learning Credit. The AOTC temporarily replaced the Hope Credit from 2009 through the end of 2012 (the Lifetime Learning Credit remains unchanged). A comparison of these two credits indicates that the AOTC is both larger—on a per capita and aggregate basis— and more widely available in comparison to the Hope Credit. Data from the Internal Revenue Service (IRS) indicates that enactment of the AOTC contributed to a more than doubling of the amount of education credits claimed by taxpayers.

Education tax credits were intended to provide federal financial assistance to students from middle-income families, who may not benefit from other forms of traditional student aid, like Pell Grants. The enactment of the AOTC reflected a desire to continue to provide substantial financial assistance to students from middle-income families, while also expanding the credit to certain lower- and upper-income students. A distributional analysis of the AOTC highlights that this benefit is targeted to the middle class, with more than half (53%) of the estimated $16 billion of AOTCs in 2009 going to taxpayers with income between $30,000 and $100,000.

One of the primary goals of education tax credits, including the AOTC, is to increase college attendance. Studies analyzing the impact education tax incentives have had on college attendance are mixed. Recent research that has focused broadly on education tax incentives that lower tuition costs and have been in effect for several years, including the Hope and Lifetime Learning Credits, found that while these credits did increase attendance by approximately 7%, 93% of recipients of these benefits would have attended college in their absence. Even though the AOTC differs from the Hope Credit in key ways, there are a variety of factors that suggest this provision may also have a limited impact on increasing college attendance. In addition, a recent report from the Treasury Department's Inspector General for Tax Administration (TIGTA) identified several compliance issues with the AOTC.

There are a variety of policy options Congress may consider regarding the AOTC, including extending the credit, extending a modified AOTC, or repealing the Hope and Lifetime Credits and extending a modified AOTC that includes provisions included in these credits. Alternatively, Congress may want to examine alternative ways to reduce the cost of higher education.

Contents

Figures

Tables

Appendixes

Contacts

Introduction

The American Opportunity Tax Credit (AOTC) is a temporary tax provision that provides financial assistance to taxpayers whose children (or who themselves) are attending college. The AOTC is scheduled to expire at the end of 2012, at which point Congress may allow the provision to expire, extend the provision in its current form, or extend a modified version of the AOTC. In light of increased congressional interest in reforming the tax code, policymakers may choose to consider modifying the AOTC in conjunction with other education tax benefits.[1] The Joint Committee on Taxation (JCT) estimated that education tax benefits cost $18.2 billion in 2012, of which $8.3 billion (46%) was attributed to the AOTC.[2]

This report provides both an in-depth description of this tax credit and an analysis of its economic impact. This report is structured to first provide an overview of the AOTC, followed by a legislative history that highlights the evolution of education tax credits from proposals in the 1960s through the extension of the AOTC in 2010. This report then analyzes the credit by looking at who claims the credit, the effect education tax credits have on increasing college attendance, and administrative issues with the AOTC. Finally, this report concludes with a brief overview of various policy options.

Current Law

The American Opportunity Tax Credit (AOTC) allows eligible taxpayers to reduce their federal income taxes by up to $2,500 per eligible student. The credit was enacted as part of the American Recovery and Reinvestment Act of 2009 (P.L. 111-5), temporarily replacing the Hope Credit for 2009 and 2010. As outlined in **Table 1**, the AOTC modified several parameters of the Hope Credit. The AOTC was extended for 2011 and 2012 by the Tax Relief, Unemployment Insurance Reauthorization, and Job Creation Act of 2010 (P.L. 111-312). Under current law, beginning in 2013[3] taxpayers will no longer be able to claim the AOTC. Taxpayers may still be eligible to claim either the Hope Credit or the Lifetime Learning Credit, both permanent tax provisions.

---

[1] For more information on current education tax benefits, see CRS Report R41967, *Higher Education Tax Benefits Brief Overview and Budgetary Effects*, by Margot L. Crandall-Hollick.

[2] Joint Committee on Taxation, *Estimates of Federal Tax Expenditures for Fiscal Years 2011-2015*, January 17, 2012, JCS-1-12.

[3] Practically, this means that taxpayers will no longer be able to claim the AOTC on their 2013 federal income tax return, generally filed in April 2014.

Table 1. Comparison of the AOTC and the HOPE Higher Education Tax Credits

Parameter	AOTC (2009-2012)	Hope Credit (Post-2012)
Maximum Value per Student	$2,500	$1,800[a]
Credit Formula	100% of the first $2,000 in qualifying expenses + 25% of the next $2,000 in qualifying expenses. The value of the expenses is *not* indexed for inflation.	100% of the first $1,200 in qualifying expenses + 50% of the next $1,200 in qualifying expenses.[a] The value of the expenses is indexed for inflation. The base level of qualified expenses is $1,000.
Income Phase-out Range	$80,000-$90,000 $160,000-$180,000 (married joint filers) The phase-out levels are not indexed for inflation.	$48,000-$58,000[a] $96,000-$116,000 (married joint filers) The phase-out levels are indexed for inflation. The base phase-out levels are $40,000-$50,000 and $80,000-$100,000 (married joint filers).
Refundability of Credit	40% of the credit is refundable. Eligible taxpayers can receive up to $1,000 as a refund.	Non-refundable
Qualifying Expenses	Tuition and required enrollment fees Course-related books, supplies and equipment	Tuition and required enrollment fees
Qualifying Education Level	First 4 years of post-secondary education	First 2 years of post-secondary education
Type of Degree Required	Student must be pursuing a degree or other recognized education credential.	Same
Number of Required Courses	Student must be enrolled at least half-time for one academic period which begins in the applicable tax year.	Same
Ineligibility Based on Felony Drug Conviction	Students with a felony drug conviction on their record are ineligible for the credit.	Same

Source: Internal Revenue Service, *Publication 970: Tax Benefits for Education 2010* and Internal Revenue Service, *Publication 970: Tax Benefits for Education 2008.*

Notes: For the 2008 and 2009 tax years, as a result of The Heartland Disaster Tax Relief Act of 2008 (included in P.L. 110-343), taxpayers in Midwestern disaster areas were eligible to claim Hope or Lifetime Learning Credits that were double the regular value of the credits. Hence, in 2009, taxpayers could elect to claim the larger Hope Credit instead of the AOTC. The Hope Credit for taxpayers in Midwestern disaster areas was calculated as 100% of the first $2,400 of qualified expenses, plus 50% of the next $2,400, resulting in a maximum Hope Credit of $3,600. For more information, see http://www.irs.gov/newsroom/article/0,,id=203082,00.html.

a. The numeric parameters for the Hope Credit reflect the values as of 2008, the most recent year for which the credit was in effect. The credit is scheduled to return in 2013, at which time the annual limit and income phase-out ranges will be adjusted for inflation.

Calculating the Credit

The AOTC is calculated as 100% of the first $2,000 of qualifying education expenses plus 25% of the next $2,000 of qualifying education expenses for each eligible student. Hence, to claim the maximum value of the credit, an eligible student will need to have incurred at least $4,000 in qualifying education expenses. The AOTC phases out for taxpayers with income[4] above certain thresholds. Specifically, the AOTC begins to phase out when income exceeds $80,000 ($160,000 for married taxpayers filing jointly[5]) and is completely phased out when income exceeds $90,000 ($180,000 for married taxpayers filing jointly). Thus, taxpayers with income over $90,000 ($180,000 or more for married taxpayers filing jointly) are be ineligible for the AOTC.

The AOTC is partially refundable, meaning taxpayers with little to no tax liability may still be able to benefit from this tax provision. A tax credit is *partially* refundable if, in cases where the credit is larger than the taxpayer's tax liability, the Internal Revenue Service (IRS) only refunds *part* of the difference. The refundable portion of the AOTC is calculated as 40% of the value of the credit the taxpayer is eligible for based on qualifying education expenses. Therefore, if the taxpayer was eligible for $2,500 of the AOTC, but had no tax liability, they could still receive $1,000 (40% of $2,500) as a refund. For an example on how to calculate the AOTC, see **Appendix B**.

Eligibility Requirements

There are a variety of limitations concerning who can claim the AOTC and what expenses can be used to claim the credit. These provisions are outlined below.

Qualifying Student

A qualifying student is either the taxpayer, the taxpayer's spouse, or an individual whom a taxpayer can claim as a dependent[6] (in many cases, the taxpayer's child). Other requirements include the following:

- **Years of Postsecondary Education:** The student must be in their first four years of post-secondary education, which for most students is the first four years of undergraduate education.[7] In addition, a taxpayer cannot claim the AOTC for a student if they have claimed education credits (AOTC, Hope, or Lifetime Learning) for the same student for four or more years.[8]

---

[4] Income is, for the purposes of the AOTC, Modified Adjusted Gross Income (MAGI), which is adjusted gross income (AGI) modified by adding back the value of (if applicable) the foreign earned income exclusion, the foreign housing exclusion, the foreign housing deduction, and the exclusion of income by bona fide residents of American Samoa or Puerto Rico.

[5] Taxpayers who file their tax returns as "married filing separately" cannot claim the AOTC.

[6] Taxpayers must claim an exemption on their tax returns for dependents who are eligible students in order to claim the credit.

[7] In addition, a taxpayer can only claim the AOTC for four calendar years per student, even if it takes the student more than four calendar years to complete their undergraduate education.

[8] For example, if a taxpayer claimed the Lifetime Learning Credit for a student for four years—perhaps for non-degree coursework—they could not then claim the AOTC for the same student, even if they were in the first four years of undergraduate education.

- **Type of Degree:** The student must be enrolled in a program that results in a degree or certificate. The credit cannot be claimed for courses that do not result in a degree or certificate. For example, it cannot be used for coursework that is used to improve jobs skills.

- **Number of Courses:** The student must be enrolled at least half time for at least one academic period (e.g., semester, trimester, quarter, or other period of study like a summer school session), which began in the tax year in which the credit is claimed. (Note that tax years are equivalent to calendar years for the purposes of federal individual income taxes.)

- **Felony Drug Conviction:** The student must not have been convicted of any state or federal felony offense for possessing or distributing a controlled substance when they claim the credit.

Qualifying Education Expenses

Qualifying education expenses are tuition and certain expenses required for enrollment at a higher education institution, including the cost of books, supplies, and equipment needed for a student's studies.

A variety of common higher education expenses *do not qualify* for the AOTC (even if the educational institution requires such payments for attendance), including

- room and board;

- insurance;

- medical expenses (including student health fees);

- transportation; and

- similar personal, living, or family expenses.

There are a variety of other requirements for education expenses used to claim the AOTC. First, qualifying education expenses used to claim the AOTC cannot generally be used to claim other education tax benefits.[9] Second, qualifying education expenses must be reduced by the entire amount of tax-free education assistance, if that assistance can be used to pay for expenses that qualify for the AOTC.[10,11] For example if a taxpayer has $2,000 in qualifying tuition payments, but receives $500 in veterans' educational assistance (which are generally tax-free), their qualifying education expenses for the AOTC are $1,500. Importantly, to the extent that the taxpayer reports a grant, scholarship or fellowship on their tax return (and hence it is subject to taxation), they do not need to reduce their education expenses by the amount of the award. Third, qualifying expenses that are claimed in a given tax year must be incurred in that tax year. Those expenses must be for an academic period that begins either in the tax year for which the credit is

---

[9] Specifically, (1) the above-the-line tuition and fees deduction; (2) the Lifetime Learning Credit; (3) the tax-free distributions from 529 qualified tuition plans (QTPs) and Coverdell Education Savings Accounts; and (4) other deductions for higher education expenses on a taxpayer's income tax return, for example, as a business expense.

[10] Tax-free education assistance includes tax-free scholarships and fellowships, Pell grants, employer-provided educational assistance, or veterans' educational assistance.

[11] Taxpayers do not need to reduce qualified expenses if part or all of them are paid for by a loan, a gift, an inheritance, or a withdrawal from the student's personal savings.

claimed, or for an academic period that begins in the first three months of the following year.[12] Finally, if any of the expenses used to calculate the credit value are refunded to the eligible student or taxpayer, even if they are refunded after the taxpayer files a tax return, the taxpayer must recalculate the value of the credit.

Legislative History

Higher education tax credits—first *enacted* in 1997 by the Taxpayer Relief Act (P.L. 105-34)—originated decades earlier in the 1960s when Congress was considering federal financial support for higher education. During consideration of the Higher Education Act of 1965 (HEA; P.L. 89-329)—which provided financial assistance to low-income Americans in the form of grants, work study, and loans[13]—"college tuition credits evolved as an alternative to financial aid programs."[14] The Johnson Administration opposed tuition credits believing that they would result in reduced revenues that could have otherwise been used for financial aid programs for the lowest-income Americans.[15] They also believed the credit would have a limited impact in influencing whether a student did or did not attend college. According to media reports, then-Treasury Secretary Stanley Surrey stated that

> a tax credit for higher education "would not result in even a single additional student going to college." The $1 billion or so that the Treasury would lose in revenue by providing a credit or several hundred dollars annually to the parents of college students can be put to better use in the form of direct financial assistance to young people who would not otherwise get to college at all.[16]

In the late 1970s, Congress again considered higher education tax credits.[17] At the time, college costs had risen sharply and many middle-class families were not eligible for federal financial aid programs to mitigate these costs. Ultimately, Congress did not enact higher education tax credits and instead expanded existing federal student aid programs, raising the income limits so that more middle-income families would qualify.[18]

Nearly two decades later, in a 1996 commencement address at Princeton University, President Clinton outlined a proposal that would later become the Hope Credit, stressing that additional education beyond high school was the key to prosperity for Americans. President Clinton

---

[12] For example, if in December 2011 a taxpayer pays $3,000 of qualified tuition for their child's spring 2012 semester which begins in February 2012, they can use that $3,000 worth of expenses to claim the AOTC on their 2011 tax return.

[13] For more information on the Higher Education Act, see CRS Report RL34214, *A Primer on the Higher Education Act (HEA)*, by Blake Alan Naughton.

[14] Benjamin Rue Silliman, "Federal Tax Policy in the Making: 32 Year to Enact College Tuition Tax Credits," *Review of Business*, vol. 23, no. 1 (Winter 2002), pp. 38-44.

[15] "Scholarships Featured in College Aid Bill," *CQ Almanac 1965*, 21st ed., pp. 294-305, http://library.cqpress.com/cqalmanac/cqal65-1259145.

[16] Eileen Shanahan, "Tax Withholding May Be Revised: Administration Studies Plan to Reduce Underpayments—Aid Unlikely This Year," *The New York Times*, March 8, 1965, p. 1.

[17] For example, see in the 95th Congress, H.R. 12050, the Tuition Tax Relief Act; H.R. 11746, the College Tuition Tax Credit Act; and S. 2142, the Tuition Tax Credit Act.

[18] See Benjamin Rue Silliman, "Federal Tax Policy in the Making: 32 Year to Enact College Tuition Tax Credits," *Review of Business*, vol. 23, no. 1 (Winter 2002), pp. 38-44.

believed that it was essential to make the 13th and 14th years of education as universal as the first 12 years. To make these first two years of higher education affordable, President Clinton proposed the creation of the Hope Credit. The credit would be structured so that "if you work hard and earn a B average in high school, we [the federal government] will give you a tax credit to pay the cost of two years of tuition at the average community college."[19] This credit was modeled on and took its name from Georgia's Help Outstanding Pupils Educationally (HOPE) Scholarship, which entitles students in Georgia with at least a B average in high school to a scholarship that covers tuition expenses at state universities and colleges.[20] (The Georgia Hope Scholarship is not a tax credit—it is a direct spending program that is not tied to Georgia's state tax system.) Some experts voiced concerns that the main purpose of education tax credits was to provide a tax cut that would be popular with voters, rather than actually increase college attendance.[21]

Ultimately, the Hope Credit was enacted as part of the Taxpayer Relief Act of 1997 (P.L. 105-34), a law that included numerous other tax cutting provisions. The Hope Credit (the key parameters of this provision are outlined in **Table 1**) provided eligible taxpayers with up to a $1,500 credit (adjusted for inflation) for tuition expenses for the first two years of higher education. Notably, the requirement that students maintain a B average in high school for eligibility was dropped. Beyond those first two years of higher education, the Taxpayer Relief Act of 1997 also created the Lifetime Learning Credit (see **Appendix A** for more information on this credit)—but for many taxpayers the value of the Lifetime Learning Credit was less than the Hope Credit.[22]

In 2008, then-candidate Barack Obama proposed replacing the Hope and Lifetime Learning Credits with the American Opportunity Tax Credit (AOTC). As originally proposed during the presidential campaign, the AOTC would be a credit equal to up to $4,000 (100% of the first $4,000 of qualifying higher education expenses) annually.[23,24] Crucially, the proposed credit was

---

[19] Princeton University, "President William J. Clinton Commencement Address," June 4, 1996, http://www.clintonlibrary.gov/assets/storage/Research%20-%20Digital%20Library/Reed-Education/91/647429-hope-scholarships-2.pdf.

[20] For more information, see Joint Committee on Taxation, *Analysis of Proposed Tax Incentives for Higher Education, Prepared for March 5 Hearing by House Ways and Means Committee*, March 4, 1997, JCS-3-97.

[21] Douglas Lederman, "The Politicking and Policy Making Behind a $40-Billion Windfall," *Chronicle of Higher Education*, vol. 44, no. 14 (November 28, 1997).

[22] The Lifetime Learning Credit provides a non-refundable tax credit for tuition and required fees that is equal to 20% of the first $10,000 in qualified tuition and related expenses *per taxpayer* (unlike the Hope Credit which is calculated *per student*). Between 1998 to 2002, the credit was equal to 20% of the first $5,000 of qualified tuition and related expenses. Hence between 1998 and 2002, the maximum value of the Lifetime Learning Credit was $1,000 per taxpayer, whereas the maximum value of the Hope Credit was $1,500 per student. The maximum amount of qualified tuition and related expenses used to calculate the Lifetime Learning Credit is not indexed for inflation, whereas the level of expenses used to calculate the Hope Credit is indexed for inflation. In 2008, the last year both the Hope Credit and the Lifetime Learning Credit were in effect, the maximum value of the Hope Credit was $1,800 per student and the maximum value of the Lifetime Learning Credit was $2,000 per taxpayer. In 2008, if total qualified education expenses were less than $9,000, most taxpayers would benefit more from the Hope Credit.

[23] For more information, see "Obama Says Tax Plan Offers More Tax Cuts; Some Analysts Question Revenue Estimates," *Bloomberg BNA Daily Tax Report*, August 29, 2008 and http://www.finaid.org/educators/presidentialcandidates.phtml.

[24] In 2008 presidential campaign documents, then-candidate Obama did not indicate the duration of the credit. According to a 2007 speech, candidate Obama stated: "I'll create a new and fully refundable tax credit worth $4,000 for tuition and fees every year, which will cover two-thirds of the tuition at the average public college or university." For more information, see Obama for America, "In Major Policy Speech, Obama Announces Plan to Reclaim the American Dream, Bettendorf IA," press release, November 7, 2007, http://www.presidency.ucsb.edu/ws/index.php?pid=93290#axzz1x7TOkCk9.

fully refundable, meaning that certain taxpayers with no tax liability—which includes many low-income Americans—would be able to benefit from this provision and receive up to $4,000 as a refund. In addition, the proposed credit would be computed by the IRS using a taxpayer's previous year tax data and provided directly to the higher education institution, not the taxpayer. Students who benefited from the credit would be required to perform 100 hours of community service when they had completed their education.[25]

On a per capita basis, the value of the AOTC, as enacted ($2,500) as part of the American Recovery and Reinvestment Act (ARRA; P.L. 111-5), was not as large as originally proposed ($4,000), but it was a larger tax benefit than the Hope Credit ($1,800), which it replaced for 2009 and 2010. (The AOTC replaces the Hope Credit, but does not affect the Lifetime Learning Credit.) For more information on key parameters of the AOTC, see **Table 1**. The AOTC as enacted had a maximum value of $2,500 and was partially refundable. Taxpayers with little or no tax liability were eligible to receive a part of the credit—40% of its value—as a refund. In addition, unlike the Obama-proposed AOTC, the actual credit did not go directly to educational institutions but instead was claimed by eligible households based on their qualifying education expenses. Finally, the community service requirement was not included as a provision of the final credit. The AOTC was extended for 2011 and 2012 by the Tax Relief, Unemployment Insurance Reauthorization, and Job Creation Act of 2010 (P.L. 111-312).

Analysis

The enactment of the AOTC has resulted in a substantial increase in the amount of education credits claimed by taxpayers, as illustrated in **Figure 1**. The increase in education tax credits underscores a broader trend, which began in 1997, of providing federal financial assistance for higher education through the tax code.[26] In light of the budgetary implications of the AOTC, it is important to explore the economic impact of this provision.

---

[25] "Obama Says Tax Plan Offers More Tax Cuts; Some Analysts Question Revenue Estimates," *BNA Daily Tax Report*, August 29, 2008.

[26] For more information, see Elaine Maag, David Mundel, and Lois Rice, et al., *Subsidizing Higher Education through Tax and Spending Programs*, Tax Policy Center, Tax Policy Issues and Options No 18, May 2007.

Figure 1. Amount of Education Tax Credits Claimed from 1998-2009

(Real 2009 $)

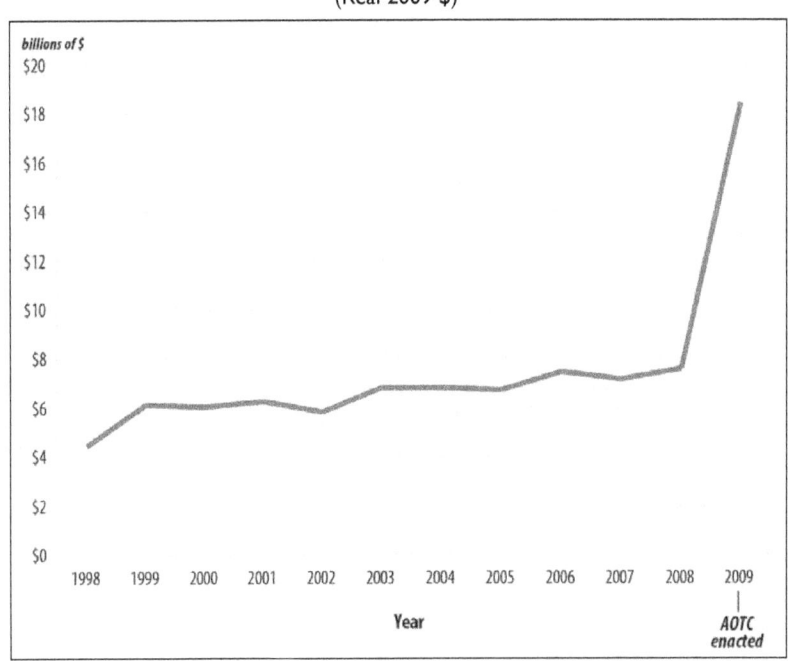

Source: Internal Revenue Service, Statistics of Information (SOI), Table 3.3

The following sections provide an economic analysis of the AOTC. They include an examination of who claims the credit, its effectiveness in boosting college attendance, and a discussion of administrative issues concerning the AOTC. Analysis of who claims the AOTC indicates that it tends to provide the greatest benefit to middle-income and upper-middle-income taxpayers. From an economic standpoint, the AOTC is an effective tax policy if it causes individuals to engage in a desired behavior—in this case attending college. Research suggests that the presence of the AOTC is *not* a major factor in increasing college attendance, especially for middle- and upper-middle-income taxpayers who are its primary beneficiaries. Hence, this credit may not be influencing behavior for many recipients and instead may be rewarding or providing a windfall to many taxpayers that would have gone to college or sent their children to college absent the credit. In addition, the Treasury Inspector General for Tax Administration (TIGTA) has identified administrative issues with the AOTC and its predecessor, the Hope Credit.

Who Benefits from the AOTC?

When education tax credits were first enacted in 1997, they were expressly intended to provide financial assistance to middle-income taxpayers.[27] Data confirms that the AOTC, like the Hope Credit, primarily benefits middle-income taxpayers, although the AOTC is also available to certain lower-income and upper-income taxpayers who were ineligible for the Hope Credit.

---

[27] Douglas Lederman, "The Politicking and Policy Making Behind a $40-Billion Windfall," *Chronicle of Higher Education*, vol. 44, no. 14 (November 28, 1997), p. A28.

Figure 2 illustrates the distribution of both the Hope Credit and the AOTC by income levels, underscoring that these tax credits provide the majority of their benefits to taxpayers with income between $30,000 and $100,000. Specifically, in 2008, approximately 75.8% of the total amount of the Hope Credit was claimed by taxpayers with income between $30,000 and $100,000, while 54.0% of the total amount of the AOTC was claimed by taxpayers in this income class. Notably, in comparison to the Hope Credit, the reduction of the share of the AOTC claimed by taxpayers in this income class resulted from both lower and upper income taxpayers claiming greater shares of the AOTC. The AOTC's modification of two components of the Hope Credit resulted in an expansion of the AOTC credit to certain low- and upper-income taxpayers.[28]

Figure 2. Share of the AOTC and Hope Credit, by Income

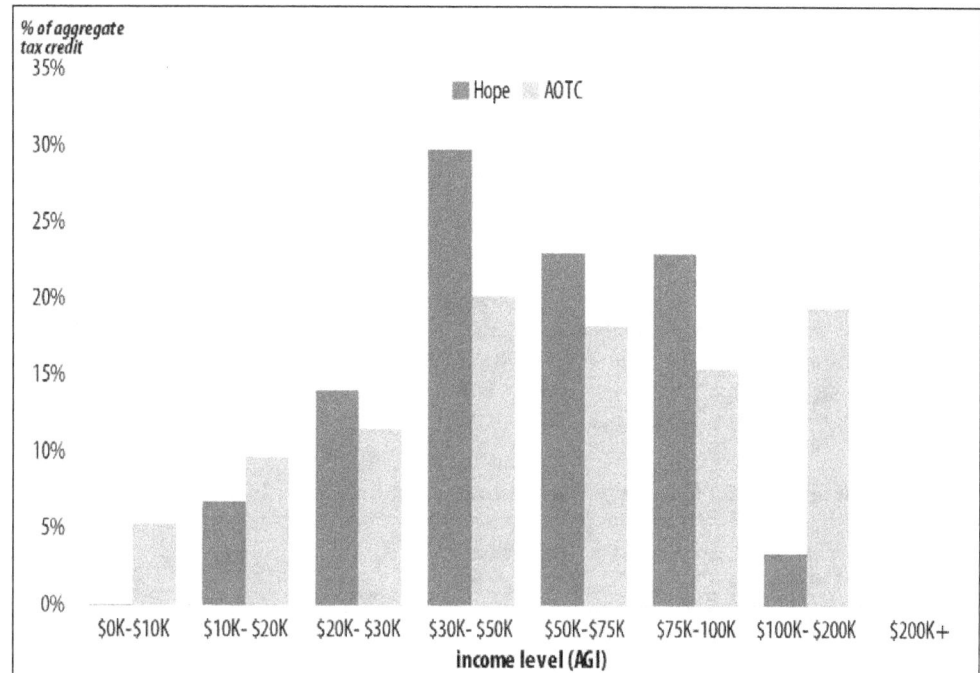

Source: CRS Calculations using IRS Statistics of Income (SOI), Table 3.3 and 2008 and 2009 Estimated Data Line Counts of Individual Income Tax Returns.

Notes: The data reflect the total amount of the Hope Credit claimed by taxpayers in 2008 and the total amount of the AOTC claimed by taxpayers in 2009. The AOTC data include the refundable portion of the credit.

The first component of the AOTC, which expanded its availability beyond middle-income taxpayers in comparison to the Hope Credit—in this case to low-income taxpayers—was its partial refundability. The Hope Credit was generally not available to lower-income taxpayers because it was non-refundable. Tax credits reduce tax liability dollar for dollar of the value of the credit, but by definition cannot reduce tax liability below zero. Hence to benefit from the credit, a

---

[28] Notably, one parameter of the AOTC that limits its availability to lower-income taxpayers remains unchanged from the Hope Credit. Specifically, both the AOTC and the Hope Credit must be reduced by tax-free educational assistance, including Pell Grants, which generally benefit low-income students and their families.[28] Since the value of the credit depends on the total amount of qualifying expenses, then all else being equal, reducing the amount of qualifying expenses reduces the value of the credit amount for taxpayers who receive tax-free educational assistance.

taxpayer must have sufficient income to owe taxes. Many low-income taxpayers did not have sufficient income to claim the Hope Credit as illustrated by **Figure 2**. In 2008, taxpayers with income under $10,000 received 0.0% of Hope Credits, while taxpayers with income between $10,000 and $20,000 received 6.8% of Hope Credits.

In contrast, the AOTC is partially refundable such that taxpayers can receive up to 40% of the value of their AOTC—a maximum of $1,000—as a refund, even if they have no tax liability.[29] In 2009, taxpayers with income under $10,000 received 5.3% of the AOTC, while taxpayers with income between $10,000 and $20,000 received 9.7% of the AOTC. As further underscored in **Table 2**, partial refundability of the tax credit benefits certain low-income taxpayers who may have been unable to benefit from the Hope Credit because of insufficient tax liability. For example, almost half (an estimated 48.1%) of the refundable portion of the AOTC is claimed by taxpayers with less than $20,000 of income. In contrast, a little over a tenth (an estimated 11.5%) of the refundable portion of the AOTC is claimed by taxpayers with incomes between $50,000 and $200,000.

The second component of the AOTC which expanded its availability beyond middle-income taxpayers in comparison to the Hope Credit—in this case to higher-income taxpayers—was increasing the income level at which the credit phased out. Certain upper-income taxpayers were ineligible for claiming the Hope Credit because the credit was unavailable to taxpayers with income above $58,000 ($116,000 for married joint filers) in 2008 (the most recent year that the Hope Credit was in effect). As illustrated by **Figure 2**, approximately 3.4% of the Hope Credit was claimed by taxpayers with income between $100,000 and $200,000. In contrast, the AOTC is available to taxpayers with income up to $90,000 ($180,000 for married joint filers). According to estimates provided in **Table 2**, in 2009 taxpayers with income between $100,000 and $200,000 claimed an estimated $3.2 billion of the credit (19.4% of the total amount of the AOTC).

Table 2. Share of AOTC Received by Taxpayers at Different Income Levels, 2009

Income (AGI)	AOTC That Offsets Tax Liability		AOTC Received as a Refund		Total AOTC		Total Income Tax Liability	
	Amount (millions)	% of Total	Amount (millions)	% of Total	Amount (millions)	% of Total	Amount (millions)	% of Total
$0-$10K	$25	0.2%	$840	21.6%	$865	5.3%	$2,139	0.2%
$10K-$20K	$543	4.4%	$1,031	26.5%	$1,574	9.7%	$5,132	0.6%
$20K-$30K	$1,127	9.1%	$750	19.3%	$1,877	11.5%	$13,433	1.5%
$30K-$50K	$2,471	20.0%	$821	21.1%	$3,292	20.2%	$49,942	5.5%
$50K-$75K	$2,628	21.2%	$346	8.9%	$2,974	18.3%	$83,857	9.2%
$75K-$100K	$2,431	19.7%	$87	2.2%	$2,518	15.5%	$85,745	9.4%
$100K-$200K	$3,145.	25.4%	$16	0.4%	$3,161	19.4%	$223,489	24.5%

[29] The refundable portion of the AOTC is calculated by first calculating the tentative value of the AOTC based on expenses and then multiplying this figure by 40%. However, some taxpayers actually use what is technically the "refundable" portion of the credit to offset tax liability. The IRS provides data on the amount of the refundable portion of the AOTC which is used to offset taxes, instead of being received as a refund. This data is combined with the non-refundable portion of the AOTC to estimate the amount of AOTC which offsets tax liability.

Income (AGI)	AOTC That Offsets Tax Liability		AOTC Received as a Refund		Total AOTC		Total Income Tax Liability	
	Amount (millions)	% of Total	Amount (millions)	% of Total	Amount (millions)	% of Total	Amount (millions)	% of Total
$200K+	$0	0.0%	$0	0.0%	$0	0.0%	447,244	49.1%
Total	$12,369	100.0%	$3,891	100.0%	$16,260	100.0%	$910,981	100.0%

Source: CRS Calculations using IRS Statistics of Income (SOI), Table 3.3 and 2009 Estimated Data Line Counts of Individual Income Tax Returns.

Notes: Items may not sum due to rounding. The IRS provides data on the total amount of non-refundable education credits claimed by AGI, which counts both the AOTC and the Lifetime Learning Credit. The IRS also provides data on the percentage of the overall amount of non-refundable education credits attributable to the AOTC and the Lifetime Learning credits. This data is used to calculate the portion of non-refundable credits attributable to the AOTC, a simplifying assumption that might not reflect the actual breakdown between these credits at different income levels.

Although a greater share of the AOTC is available to low- and high-income taxpayers in comparison to the Hope Credit, data suggest (see **Figure 2**) that the AOTC has shifted more of its benefits to higher-income taxpayers. For example, approximately 15% of the AOTC was claimed by taxpayers with income under $20,000, more than double the share of the Hope Credit (6.8%) claimed by taxpayers in this income class. In contrast, approximately 19.4% of the AOTC was claimed by taxpayers with income between $100,000 and $200,000, more than five times the share of the Hope Credit (3.4%) claimed by taxpayers in this income class. Notably, these gains were accompanied by the reduction in the shares of the AOTC (in comparison to the Hope Credit) that went to taxpayers with income between $20,000 and $100,000.

Given that children of taxpayers at the upper end of income scale are more likely to attend college than their lower-income counterparts,[30] providing education incentives to these taxpayers may not increase college enrollment, but instead reward behavior that would have occurred absent the incentive.

Does the AOTC Increase College Attendance?

One of the primary goals[31] of the AOTC is to increase college attendance.[32] Increased college attendance may not only lead to benefits for individuals in terms of higher wages, but also may

---

[30] For more information, see Elaine Maag and Katie Fitzpatrick, "Federal Financial Aid for Higher Education: Programs and Prospects," The Urban Institute, January 1, 2004, pp. 5-6, http://www.urban.org/uploadedPDF/ 410996_federal_financial_aid.pdf. In addition, research from the U.S. Department of Education indicates that "Differences in immediate college enrollment rates by family income, race/ethnicity, and sex were observed over time. In every year between 1975 and 2009, the immediate college enrollment rates of high school completers from low- and middle-income families were lower than those of high school completers from high-income families. Most recently, in 2009, the immediate college enrollment rate of high school completers from low-income families was 55 percent, 29 percentage points lower than the rate of high school completers from high-income families (84 percent). The immediate college enrollment rate of high school completers from middle-income families (67 percent) also trailed the rate of their peers from high-income families by 17 percentage points." U.S. Department of Education, National Center for Education Statistics. (2011). The Condition of Education 2011 (NCES 2011-033), Indicator 21, http://nces.ed.gov/ fastfacts/display.asp?id=51.

[31] The AOTC may have other policy objectives. For example, the AOTC, like other forms of financial aid for higher education, may also enable students to be more selective in choosing the college they will attend, allowing them to attend a more expensive institution. The credit may also increase the time a student spends in school. Finally, the (continued...)

---

provide societal benefits including increased productivity and innovation.[33,34] There are a variety of factors that may determine whether a student attends college, including family socioeconomic level, student educational aspirations, peer support, academic performance, and the cost of college.[35]

The AOTC, like other forms of traditional student aid and other forms of tax-based financial aid, subsidizes some of the costs associated with higher education and thus reduces its cost. The effect that a cost reduction has on college attendance will depend on how sensitive a student (and his family's) decision to attend college is to price. Some students will be very sensitive to price and in so far as the AOTC reduces college cost, this tax benefit will induce them to attend college. On the other hand, certain students will attend college irrespective of price. In this case, the AOTC rewards students and their families for an action—attending college—that they would have made regardless of the credit's availability, and the credit is simply a windfall gain to certain taxpayers.

Studies analyzing the effect of education tax incentives on college attendance are mixed. Because of the limited amount of data available concerning the AOTC, research has instead focused more broadly on education tax incentives that lower tuition costs and that have been in effect for several years—namely the Hope Credit, the Lifetime Learning Credit, and the above-the-line tuition and fees deduction (see **Appendix A** for more information on these tax benefits). [36] Analysis by the Congressional Budget Office (CBO) conducted two years after the Hope and Lifetime Learning Credits were enacted concluded that "tax credits are unlikely to cause

---

(...continued)

AOTC may enable students or their families to take on less debt to finance their education. Studies that have evaluated education tax incentives have not focused on these potential aspects of higher education tax credits, so they are not the focus of this report.

[32] Most studies have focused on the impact of tax credits on college attendance, but have not focused more broadly on college completion. While people who receive some college education generally earn more even if they do not graduate, the size of this effect is still being debated.

[33] This economic rationale may be referred to as the "positive externality" rationale for government interventions in higher education. Broadly, an externality is a cost or benefit associated with a transaction that is not reflected in market prices borne by the buyer or seller. In the case of a positive externality associated with education, the positive benefit to society in terms of increased productivity and innovation is greater than the benefit to the individual, which may result in under-investment in education from a social perspective. In addition to the positive social benefits discussed, increased education is also correlated with reduced reliance on government assistance programs, less crime, and greater civic participation. For more information, see Elaine Maag and Katie Fitzpatrick, "Federal Financial Aid for Higher Education: Programs and Prospects," *The Urban Institute*, January 1, 2004, http://www.urban.org/publications/410996.html.

[34] While one economic rationale for federal financial aid for college attendance is the "positive externality" rationale, there are other rationales for government intervention in higher education financing. First, private capital markets may be unwilling to lend to students to finance their higher education. Many students do not have sufficient savings to finance their education. And since students often lack property to pledge as collateral for student loans, private lenders must charge high interest rates to reflect the losses they would incur (and could not recover) if the student defaults. To rectify this problem, the federal government guarantees student loans which effectively absorbs private lenders default risk. A second reason the government may provide financial assistance for higher education is to expand access to college, and since college-educated workers earn more than those with a high-school diploma, to ultimately mitigate income inequality.

[35] Jacqueline E. King, "Improving the Odds: Factors that Increase the Likelihood of Four-Year College Attendance Among High School Seniors," *College Board Report No. 96-2*, 1996, http://professionals.collegeboard.com/profdownload/pdf/RR%2096-2.PDF.

[36] For more information on the Lifetime Learning Credit and the tuition and fees deduction, see CRS Report R41967, *Higher Education Tax Benefits Brief Overview and Budgetary Effects*, by Margot L. Crandall-Hollick.

---

substantial increases in college enrollment."[37] A later study echoed the CBO's conclusion, finding that the Hope and Lifetime Learning Credits had no impact on college enrollment, although there were possible limitations with the analysis.[38,39] More recent research[40] has found that tax-based aid did have an impact on college attendance, but also that a significant proportion of recipients— 93%—would have attended college in the absence of these benefits.[41]

Based on the available research and current data on who receives the AOTC, there may be several factors that limit the AOTC's impact on college attendance.

- **Income Level of Beneficiaries:** Research indicates that students from lower-income households are more sensitive to the price of college when deciding whether to attend college, in comparison to their higher-income counterparts.[42] Policies that reduce the price of college, like the AOTC, would then be expected to increase enrollment if they were targeted towards lower-income students. However, as previously discussed, the AOTC primarily benefits middle-income taxpayers, and hence may result in a windfall to many of these taxpayers.

- **Timing of Tax Benefit:** Unlike aid and loans received before or at the time of attendance, the AOTC like other education tax benefits (e.g., the Lifetime Learning Credit and tuition and fees deductions, see **Appendix A**) may be received up to 15 months after education expenses are incurred.[43] For families who have limited resources to pay education expenses up front (e.g., they have insufficient savings to pay for college costs), tax credits will provide little benefit in financing their college costs.[44] However, the AOTC

---

[37] Congressional Budget Office, *An Economic Analysis of the Taxpayer Relief Act of 1997*, CBO Paper, April 2000, p. 20, http://www.cbo.gov/publication/12200.

[38] Bridget T. Long, "The Impact of Federal Tax Credits for Higher Education Expenses," *National Bureau of Economic Research*, September 2004, p. 137.

[39] According to the Government Accountability Office, there were a variety of limitations to the study by Bridget Long (see above) including that "the study measured eligibility for the credits rather than the receipt of tax credits. Measuring eligibility rather the receipt of credits tends to underestimate the effects of credits on attendance because many tax filers who appear to be eligible for the credits do not claim them." See U.S. Government Accountability Office, *Student Aid and Postsecondary Tax Preferences Limited Research Exists on Effectiveness of Tools to Assist Students and Families through Title IV Student Aid and Tax Preferences*, GAO-05-684, July 2005, p. 30.

[40] Nicholas Turner, "The Effect of Tax-Based Federal Student Aid on College Enrollment," *National Tax Journal*, vol. 64, no. 3 (September 2011), pp. 839-862.

[41] Specifically, the 2011 study by Turner found that three tax benefits (the Hope Tax Credit, the Lifetime Learning Credit, and the Tuition and Fees Above-the-Line Deduction) "increases full-time enrollment in the first two years of college by about…6.7 percent." This "7 percent enrollment increase implied that 93% of tax-based aid recipients would have enrolled without the tax-based subsidy." See Nicholas Turner, "The Effect of Tax-Based Federal Student Aid on College Enrollment," *National Tax Journal*, vol. 64, no. 3 (September 2011), pp. 840 and 852.

[42] According to CBO, "empirical research indicates that tuition levels had little effect on enrollment rates of students from middle and high-income families, but they can affect students from low-income families." Congressional Budget Office, *An Economic Analysis of the Taxpayer Relief Act of 1997*, CBO Paper, April 2000, p. 20.

[43] Taxpayers could, in anticipation of receiving the tax benefit, adjust the amount of tax withheld from their pay. However, there is little evidence that taxpayers do this, likely because it increases the complexity of paying taxes.

[44] For more information, see Nicholas Turner, "The Effect of Tax-Based Federal Student Aid on College Enrollment," *National Tax Journal*, vol. 64, no. 3 (September 2011), pp. 845; Bridget T, Long, "The Impact of Federal Tax Credits for Higher Education Expenses," *National Bureau of Economic Research*, September 2004, pp. 104 and 132; and Government Accountability Office, *Student Aid and Postsecondary Tax Preferences Limited Research Exists on Effectiveness of Tools to Assist Students and Families through Title IV Student Aid and Tax Preferences*, GAO-05-684, (continued...)

---

may enable families that do receive loans to ultimately reduce their loan
balances by applying the credit amounts to loan balances.

- **Complexity of Benefit:** There are a variety of tax benefits that students or
  their families can claim when they file their taxes, including the AOTC, the
  Lifetime Learning Credit, and the tuition and fees deduction. These tax
  preferences differ in a variety of ways including eligibility criteria, benefit
  levels, and income phase-outs (see **Table 1** and **Appendix A**). The value of
  the tax benefit may also depend on the amount of student aid taxpayers or
  their children receive. Given these numerous factors, taxpayers may not
  know which tax preference provides the most benefit until they file their
  taxes—and calculating the tax benefit of each provision can "place
  substantial demands on the knowledge and skills of millions of students and
  families."[45] This complexity may result in some taxpayers choosing not to
  claim a tax benefit like the AOTC, or not claiming the tax provision that
  provides the greatest benefit. Studies have found that between 27%[46] and
  37%[47] of taxpayers failed to claim eligible education tax benefits.

- **Institutional Response:** Some experts have expressed a concern that
  colleges and universities—especially those with tuition below the maximum
  amount subsidized by education tax credits—may respond to the availability
  of education tax credits like the AOTC by increasing their tuition.[48] This
  would lessen the ability of education tax credits to lower the after-tax price of
  college. For example, if a student is eligible for a $2,000 credit, but their
  college increases tuition by $2,000, the price of college will effectively be
  unchanged and the credit will entirely benefit the college. If the college raises
  tuition for all students, irrespective of whether they are eligible for the credit,
  some students may actually see the cost of college rise. While there is
  currently no research on the institutional response to the AOTC, studies of
  the Hope and Lifetime Learning Credits have found little evidence that they
  resulted in tuition increases.[49] This may in part be due to the fact that the
  colleges most likely to raise tuition—schools with lower tuition levels like

---

(...continued)

July 2005, p. 30.

[45] Government Accountability Office, *Student Aid and Postsecondary Tax Preferences Limited Research Exists on Effectiveness of Tools to Assist Students and Families through Title IV Student Aid and Tax Preferences*, GAO-05-684, July 2005, p. 23.

[46] Government Accountability Office, *Student Aid and Postsecondary Tax Preferences Limited Research Exists on Effectiveness of Tools to Assist Students and Families through Title IV Student Aid and Tax Preferences*, GAO-05-684, July 2005, p. 21.

[47] Nicholas Turner, "The Effect of Tax-Based Federal Student Aid on College Enrollment," *National Tax Journal*, vol. 64, no. 3 (September 2011), pp. 844. In addition, one analysis found that 26% of eligible students did not claim the Hope Credit. See Leonard Burman, Elaine Maag, and Peter Orszag, et al., "The Distributional Consequences of Federal Assistance for Higher Education: The Intersection of Tax and Spending Programs," *Tax Policy Center*, August 2005, p. 15.

[48] The AOTC subsidizes the first $4,000 of tuition expenses—subsidizing 100% of the first $2,000 in tuition expenses and 25% of the next $2,000 in expenses. For a college that charges less than $2,000, they can increase tuition to $2,000 without increasing the after-tax tuition cost to taxpayers. Increasing tuition above $2,000 would lead students to face higher after-tax tuition costs.

[49] For more information, see Elaine Maag, David Mundel, and Lois Rice, et al., *Subsidizing Higher Education through Tax and Spending Programs*, Tax Policy Center, Tax Policy Issues and Options No 18, May 2007.

community colleges—predominantly service lower-income students who were ineligible for the non-refundable Hope Credit and Lifetime Learning Credit. However, insofar as the AOTC benefits certain low-income taxpayers that were ineligible for the Hope Credit, schools may choose to raise tuition levels, reducing the effective value of the AOTC and potentially increasing the after-tax cost of college for students ineligible for the AOTC.

While there are a variety of factors that may limit the ability of the AOTC to increase college attendance, research indicates that student aid generally, including traditional student aid, may have a similar impact as the AOTC on college attendance.[50] Hence, some of the limitations of the AOTC in increasing college attendance may apply more broadly to other forms of federal financial assistance.

Finally, federal financial assistance for higher education may reduce the after-tax price of college, but cost is just one factor that influences college attendance. Other factors, like college preparedness, may also influence not only whether students attend college, but whether they graduate.[51] Research indicates that college preparedness tends to be correlated with income, with lower-income students less prepared for college than their higher-income counterparts.[52] Thus, other societal factors that exist prior to college may limit the impact aid has on increasing college attendance, especially among needier students.[53]

Are Ineligible Taxpayers Erroneously Claiming the AOTC?

Taxpayers are more likely to claim tax benefits when they are simple and straightforward to claim. However, the trade-off for ease in claiming tax benefits is that it may result in increased errors—both intentional and unintentional—as illustrated in a recent Treasury Inspector General for Tax Administration (TIGTA) report on the AOTC.[54]

The 2011 TIGTA report examined 2009 income tax returns that claimed this credit and identified 2.1 million taxpayers who received $3.2 billion in AOTC credits that appeared to be erroneous. Of these potentially erroneous credits, the majority ($2.6 billion) were a result of the IRS being

---

[50] For example, one study found that increases in Pell grants increased enrollment by 5.3% for low-income students at low-cost institutions. See Bradley Curs, Larry Singell, and Glen Waddell, "Money for Nothing? The Impact of Changes in the Pell Grant Program on Institutional Revenues and the Placement of Need Students," *Education Finance and Policy*, vol. 2, no. 3 (2007), p. 231.

[51] See Martha J. Bailey and Susan M. Dynarski, "Gains and Gaps: Changing Inequality in the U.S. College Entry and Completion," *NBER Working Paper No. 17633*, December 2011, http://www.nber.org/papers/w17633.

[52] According to the Department of Education, "…among high school graduates in 1992, only 21 percent of those with family incomes of less than $25,000 were highly qualified for admission at a four-year institution, and 20 percent were minimally qualified. For students with family incomes above $75,000, 56 percent were highly qualified and 12 percent minimally qualified." U.S. Department of Education, National Center for Education Statistics, Access to Postsecondary Education for the 1992 High Schools Graduates, NCES 98-105, by Lutz Berkner and Lisa Chavez, Project Officer: C. Dennis Carroll, Washington DC: 1997, http://nces.ed.gov/pubs98/98105.pdf.

[53] Research has found that even when financial aid increases college enrollment, many of the students who attend college as a result of this assistance "are from the lower end of the ability spectrum and eventually dropout or take longer than average to complete college." Carlos Garriga and Mark P. Keightley, "A General Equilibrium Theory of College with Education Subsidies, In-School Labor Supply, and Borrowing Constraints," *Federal Reserve Bank of St. Louis Working Paper Series*, November 2007, http://research.stlouisfed.org/wp/2007/2007-051.pdf.

[54] See Treasury Inspector General for Tax Administration, *Billions of Dollars in Education Credits Appear to Be Erroneous*, September 16, 2011, http://www.treasury.gov/tigta/auditreports/2011reports/201141083fr.pdf.

---

unable to confirm that the students claimed on the taxpayers' tax returns attended a college or university.[55] TIGTA proposed that the IRS examine the feasibility of using two databases at the Department of Education to confirm that the student for whom the credit was claimed on a tax return was actually a student and eligible for the credit, although the TIGTA report noted that the databases did contain some inaccuracies. They also proposed requiring taxpayers to provide more information on their tax returns about the college or university a student attended, including information that would detail that the student was eligible for the AOTC (for example requiring the taxpayer to check a box on their tax return that indicates the student is attending the college at least half-time).

TIGTA also estimated that more than 350,000 taxpayers claimed $550 million of AOTC credits even though the information supplied to the IRS by educational institutions—the form 1098-T— indicated, according to TIGTA, that the student was ineligible for the credit. The 1098-T includes two check boxes to identify if the student is at least attending the institution half-time and if they are a graduate student. TIGTA identified graduate students as ineligible for the AOTC,[56] although the law does not actually deny the credit to graduate students. The credit is allowed for the first four years of post-secondary education, and while in most cases this will be undergraduate education, some students may be pursuing a graduate program in their fourth year of education. (In contrast, TIGTA does correctly identify that students must be enrolled at least half-time to be eligible for the credit.) In addition, TIGTA identified in their 2011 report and previous reports that educational institutions may be inaccurately filling out the 1098-T. This finding underscores that minimizing fraudulent claims of the AOTC may require additional and improved information not only from taxpayers, but from colleges and universities, as well.

The report also identified other ineligible taxpayers who erroneously claimed $88 million of credits, including taxpayers who were incarcerated for an entire year and taxpayers who claimed the AOTC for a student who was claimed as a dependent on a different taxpayer's return. Unlike other TIGTA recommendations, which required additional information from either the taxpayer or education institutions, the report recommended improving the use of available databases to check the eligibility of taxpayers.

Recently introduced legislation in the 112th Congress is intended to limit ineligible taxpayers from claiming education tax credits, including the AOTC. H.R. 4372 would deny education tax credits to taxpayers who did not provide the employer identification number of a student's educational institution. In addition, the bill would increase information sharing between the IRS and certain prison officials to combat tax fraud among prisoners.[57]

---

[55] In order to claim the AOTC (and the Lifetime Learning Credit), students must fill out and attach the IRS Form 8863 to their income tax return and include the appropriate credit amount on their tax return. In addition, both the taxpayer and the IRS receive from the college or university a form 1098-T, which has information on the educational institution, student, and payments received for qualified tuition expenses.[55] The inability of TIGTA to match tax returns which claimed the AOTC to 1098-T forms led them to conclude that these AOTC claims were likely erroneous, although the IRS disagrees with this conclusion.

[56] Treasury Inspector General for Tax Administration, *Billions of Dollars in Education Credits Appear to Be Erroneous*, September 16, 2011, http://www.treasury.gov/tigta/auditreports/2011reports/201141083fr.pdf, p.12.

[57] This bill would also disallow the credit to taxpayers if they do not provide the Social Security numbers of the students for whom they are claiming the credit. Under current law, otherwise eligible students may provide an Individual Taxpayer Identification Number (ITIN) to claim the credit.

Although minimizing the administrative burden in order to claim the AOTC may encourage eligible taxpayers to claim this benefit, it might also result in more taxpayers erroneously claiming the credit. Reducing erroneous claims may require both taxpayers and higher education institutions to provide additional information to the IRS, and may also necessitate improved compliance checks by the IRS.

Policy Options

The AOTC has temporarily replaced the Hope Credit for the past four years (2009-2012), and one policy option available to Congress is to allow the credit to expire as scheduled at the end of 2012 (although the permanent Hope and Lifetime Learning Credit will be available to eligible taxpayers). Congress may also want to consider extending the credit as is, extending a modified AOTC, or repealing the Hope and Lifetime Learning Credits and extending a modified AOTC that includes provisions included in these credits. Finally, Congress may want to consider federal financial aid for higher education holistically, which could include alternative ways to reduce the cost of higher education.

Allow the AOTC to Expire as Scheduled

Policymakers may allow the AOTC to expire as scheduled at the end of 2012, although certain taxpayers may still be eligible for the permanent Hope or Lifetime Learning Credit.[58] However, the value of these credits will generally be less than the value of the AOTC. In addition, since these credits are non-refundable and they phase out at lower income levels than the AOTC, certain taxpayers who are eligible for the AOTC may not be able to claim any education tax credit starting in 2013.

Among students for whom the AOTC is a major factor in whether they will attend college, losing the benefit or receiving a smaller Hope or Lifetime Learning Credit may result in fewer students attending college or choosing to defer attending college until it is affordable. Insofar as the AOTC is claimed by taxpayers whose children (or who themselves) would have attended college absent the availability of the AOTC, the expiration of the credit would eliminate or reduce a windfall benefit while lessening revenue losses. The most recent two-year extension[59] of the AOTC was estimated to reduce revenues by $17.6 billion over a 10-year budgetary window (2011-2020).[60]

Extend or Modify the AOTC

Policymakers may choose to extend the current AOTC or extended a modified AOTC. The President's FY2013 budget has proposed extending the credit permanently (effectively replacing

---

[58] The Hope Credit is only available for the first two years of post-secondary education, while the Lifetime Learning Credit is available for an unlimited number of years. Hence, taxpayers who claim the AOTC for at least two years for a particular student will be ineligible to claim the Hope Credit, but may be eligible to claim the Lifetime Learning Credit.

[59] The AOTC was extended for 2011 and 2012 by the Tax Relief, Unemployment Insurance Reauthorization, and Job Creation Act of 2010 (P.L. 111-312).

[60] Joint Committee on Taxation, *Estimated Budget Effects of the "Tax Relief, Unemployment.*, December 10, 2010, JCX-54-10.

the Hope Credit with the AOTC), while H.R. 3865, the College Tax Cut Extension Act of 2012, would extend the AOTC through the end of 2016.

The AOTC could also be extended but modified in a variety of ways. Policymakers may choose to either expand or limit certain parameters of the credit, for example, by using a different credit formula, changing the amount of qualifying expenses that can be used to claim the credit, adjusting the portion of the credit (currently 40%) that is refundable, modifying the income level at which the credit phases out, allowing taxpayers to claim the credit for either more or less than four years of post-secondary education, changing the definition of qualifying expenses (for example to include room and board), and providing non-degree-seeking students (such as students in job-training programs) eligibility for the credit.

If desired, certain changes to the AOTC may expand the credit's availability to lower-income recipients. For example, policymakers could make a greater percentage of the credit refundable. They could also modify the credit such that a lower level of expenses would be necessary to claim the maximum credit (for example, the formula could be 100% of the first $2,500 of qualifying expenses). In contrast, other modifications, like increasing the income level at which the credit phases out, may expand the credit to additional upper-income taxpayers. These changes may increase confusion among taxpayers, especially when trying to determine which higher education tax credit (or the above-the-line deduction for tuition and fees) provides the greatest benefit. Extension of the AOTC beyond 2012, whether in its current form or a modified form, will result in a greater budgetary cost than if the credit expired as scheduled and the Hope Credit goes back into effect.

Consolidate the AOTC with Other Education Tax Benefits

Policymakers may instead choose to consolidate the AOTC with other education tax incentives that reduce tuition costs—the Lifetime Learning Credit and tuition and fees deduction. Prior to enactment of the AOTC, there were several legislative proposals to consolidate these tax benefits. For example, in the 109th Congress, Senator Baucus introduced the Education Competitiveness Act of 2006 (S. 3902), which repealed the Hope and Lifetime Learning Credits and replaced them with a fully refundable $2,000 higher education tax credit. In the 110th Congress, the bipartisan Universal Higher Education and Lifetime Learning Act of 2007 (H.R. 2458) consolidated the Hope and Lifetime Learning Credits and the tuition and fees deduction into one partially refundable credit with a maximum value of $3,000 (50% or up to $1,500 was available as a refund). In addition, this legislation set a lifetime limit of $12,000 per student for the credit (the credit could be claimed for no more than two years of graduate education). The budgetary impact of consolidating higher education tax benefits into one credit is unknown, but could be designed to increase revenue, decrease revenue, or remain revenue neutral.

Alternative Policies to Reduce the Cost of Higher Education

The AOTC is one of a variety of policies designed to lower the cost of education to students and their families and hence increase accessibility to higher education. Policymakers may pursue several options concerning the AOTC. Alternatively, they may choose to re-evaluate the federal government's role in higher education financing more broadly by considering education tax incentives like the AOTC in context with other forms of federal financial aid to develop a broader higher education financing policy. For example, policymakers could expand the types of expenses that would qualify for the AOTC such that a low-income student who uses a Pell Grant to pay for most or all of their tuition could still benefit from the AOTC. Or policymakers may choose to reformulate the federal government's role in higher education financing entirely by encouraging alternative financing mechanisms like human capital contracts,[61] which allow a student to repay an investor a percentage of future earnings for a fixed period of time. Although there may be shortfalls with this particular proposal,[62] approaching higher education policy holistically— instead of tax policy versus traditional financial aid—may provide more benefit to low- and middle-income students.

---

[61] For more information on human capital contracts, see http://www.cato.org/pubs/pas/pa462.pdf and http://opinionator.blogs.nytimes.com/2011/05/30/instead-of-student-loans-investing-in-futures/.

[62] For example, human capital contracts, which theoretically work best when there is some predictability on a student's future wages, would tend to provide greater financing to students who pursue profitable careers. For other professions, especially ones that may not yield economic returns to students—like working in a developing economy—human capital contracts may not be an effective financing mechanism. In addition, human capital contracts may suffer from a problem economists refer to as "asymmetric information." The student may say he is pursuing a degree to become a lawyer, but instead may wish to pursue teaching as a career. The investor will hence receive less than they would have expected.

Appendix A. Other Tax Provisions For Current-Year Higher Education Expenses

Under current law, there are a variety of benefits available to taxpayers for current-year higher education expenses. A complete list can be found in CRS Report R41967, *Higher Education Tax Benefits: Brief Overview and Budgetary Effects*, by Margot L. Crandall-Hollick.

Of these benefits, the AOTC, the Hope Credit, the Lifetime Learning Credit, and the above-the-line deduction for tuition and fees[63] are often discussed together as the main tax benefits for current-year higher education expenses. A taxpayer cannot claim both the deduction and an education credit (Lifetime Learning or AOTC) for the same student in the same year. Details on the Lifetime Learning Credit and the tuition and fees deduction are provided below.

Table A-1. Key Parameters of the Lifetime Learning Credit and the Tuition and Fees Deduction

	Lifetime Learning Credit	Tuition and Fees Deduction
Type of Benefit	Tax credit	Above-the-line deduction from gross income
Maximum Value	$2,000 credit per taxpayer	$4,000 deduction per student
Credit Formula	20% of first $10,000 of expenses	Not applicable
Income Phase-out Range	$51,000-$61,000 (102,000-$122,000 for married joint filers) in 2011	$65,000-$80,000($130,000-$160,000 for married joint filers)
Refundability	Non-refundable	Not applicable
Qualifying Expenses	Tuition and required enrollment fees	Same
Qualifying Education Level	Post-secondary education, including coursework to acquire or improve job skills. The credit is available for an unlimited number of years.	Post-secondary education
Type of Degree Required	No degree requirement	Undergraduate or graduate degree
Number of Required Courses	No requirement	No requirement

Source: Table compiled by CRS.

---

[63] Above-the-line deductions are available to taxpayers who do not itemize their deductions. In addition, a deduction lowers taxable income, hence lowering tax liability proportionally to the taxpayer's income bracket (a $100 deduction for a taxpayer in the 25% bracket reduces tax liability by $25).

Appendix B. Calculating the AOTC: A Stylized Example

In 2011, the Smiths pay $8,000 of college expenses for Sarah. Of the $8,000 in expenses, $6,000 are for tuition and are considered qualifying expenses, while $2,000 are for room and board expenses, which are not qualifying expenses.

The Smiths' daughter Sarah attends University X in 2011. The Smiths file their tax return as married joint filers. They have a combined income of $100,000, which is below the level at which the credit begins to phase out.

To help pay for these costs, the university gives Sarah a $4,000 tax-free scholarship (i.e., none of the scholarship is subject to taxation), which can be used to pay for any part of Sarah's university expenses. The remainder of the cost is paid for with student loans. Sarah is a first-year undergraduate at University X enrolled full-time in a degree program and is eligible to claim the AOTC. She is claimed as a dependent by the Smiths.

Step 1. Qualifying Expenses: Sarah has $6,000 in qualifying expenses that are reduced by the entire value of her tax-free scholarship. Importantly, even though the tax-free scholarship can be used for expenses aside from tuition and fees, because it is tax-free, she must reduce her qualifying expenses by the total value of the award. If she had used the $4,000 award to pay for room and board (not a qualifying expense) and she had also reported it on her (or her parent's) income tax return), she would not need to reduce her qualifying expenses by the value of the award. However, because the award is entirely tax-free, her $6,000 in qualifying expenses are reduced by $4,000 and she has $2,000 in qualifying expenses.

Step 2. Calculating the AOTC: Because Sarah has $2,000 in qualifying expenses, her parents can claim a $2,000 AOTC (100% x first $2,000 of qualifying expenses).

Author Contact Information

Margot L. Crandall-Hollick
Analyst in Public Finance
mcrandallhollick@crs.loc.gov, 7-7582